W9-BVX-979

DISCARD

Prairie Numbers

An Illinois Number Book

Written by Kathy-jo Wargin and Illustrated by Kathy O'Malley

Sleeping Bear Press™
310 North Main Street, Suite 300
Chelsea, MI 48118
www.sleepingbearpress.com

THOMSON ™
GALE

© 2006 Thomson Gale, a part of the Thomson Corporation.

Thomson, Star Logo and Sleeping Bear Press are trademarks
and Gale is a registered trademark used herein under license.

Printed and bound in China.

10 9 8 7 6 5 4 3 2 1

Library of Congress Cataloging-in-Publication Data

Wargin, Kathy-jo.
Prairie numbers : an Illinois number book / written by Kathy-jo Wargin;
illustrated by Kathy O'Malley.
p. cm.
Summary: "Using numbers, readers are introduced to Illinois state symbols,
industry, animals, and more. Written for two levels, the book uses poetry and
numbers to introduce each topic. Expository text provides detailed information
about each topic"—Provided by publisher.
ISBN 1-58536-180-1
1. Illinois—Juvenile literature. 2. Counting—Juvenile literature. I. O'Malley,
Kathy. II. Title.

F541.3.W38 2006
977.3—dc22   2006004295

To children young and old—
you can always count on those you love.

KATHY-JO

❦

To my friends and family who always said, "It's either this, or 9 to 5."
I'm sure glad I chose this.

KATHY

The Shedd Aquarium opened in 1929 as the largest aquarium in the world. Named for its benefactor, John Graves Shedd, it was created with the goal of helping visitors learn about the natural world. Today the aquarium gets all of its freshwater from Lake Michigan, adding salt to mix its own saltwater. Home to more than 6,000 fishes, reptiles, amphibians, mammals, and invertebrates, it is one of the oldest public aquariums in the world.

one

1

1 big aquarium
named for John Graves Shedd.
Silly otters slip and slide,
eager to be fed.

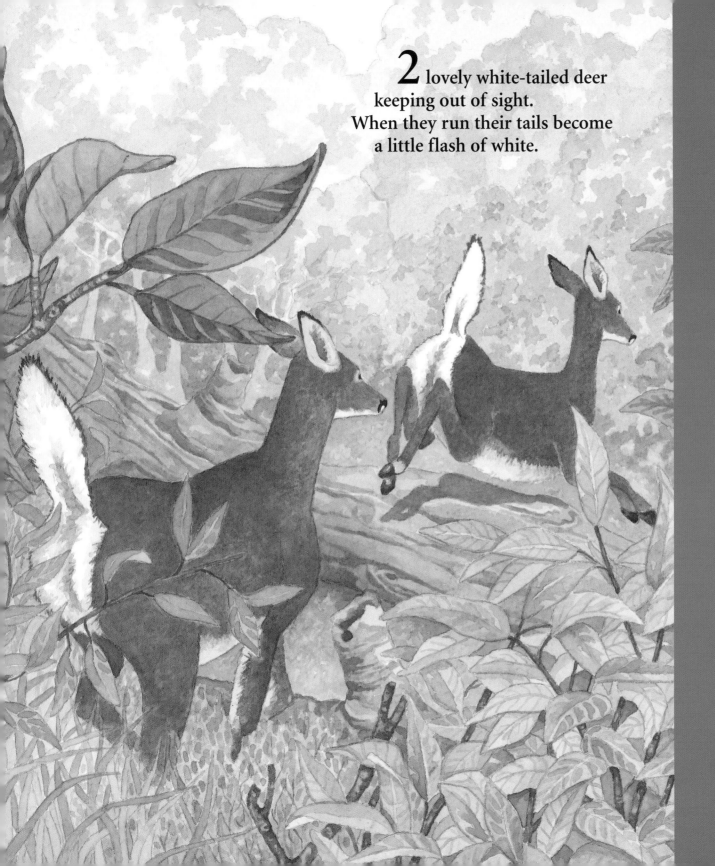

2 lovely white-tailed deer
keeping out of sight.
When they run their tails become
a little flash of white.

The white-tailed deer, or *Odocoileus virginianus*, is the Official State Animal of Illinois. Although currently abundant in Illinois, the white-tailed deer was once almost extinct in the state. Due to hunting and land use, the deer population was nearly decimated by the early 1900s.

However, restocking of deer during the 1930s helped the deer population regain its foothold, and by the 1970s, deer were present in all Illinois counties. White-tailed deer prefer a mixed habitat of wooded areas for shelter and clearings, or naturally open areas, for grazing. They eat tender shoots, leaves, and twigs.

two

2

3 painted turtles
resting in the sun.
Poking in and out of home,
can you count each one?

The Painted Turtle is the Official State Reptile of Illinois. It was chosen in 2004 as the selection for state reptile, and the honor became official in March 2005. Painted turtles are a familiar sight among the lakes, rivers, and ponds of Illinois, most often noticed when basking on logs or gathering together in groups. The painted turtle thrives on insects and other aquatic invertebrates and plants.

three
3

Popcorn was designated as the Official State Snack Food of Illinois in 2003. As one of the top popcorn-growing states in the nation, Illinois ranks fourth in acres of harvested popcorn. This means that Illinois farmers grow enough popcorn to fill more than 40 million two-pound (0.91 kilogram) bags with kernels every year.

The first commercial popping machine was invented in Illinois by Charles Cretors in 1885. Called the Automatic Self-Buttering and Salting Corn Popper, it made hot, buttery popcorn a widely available snack.

four

4

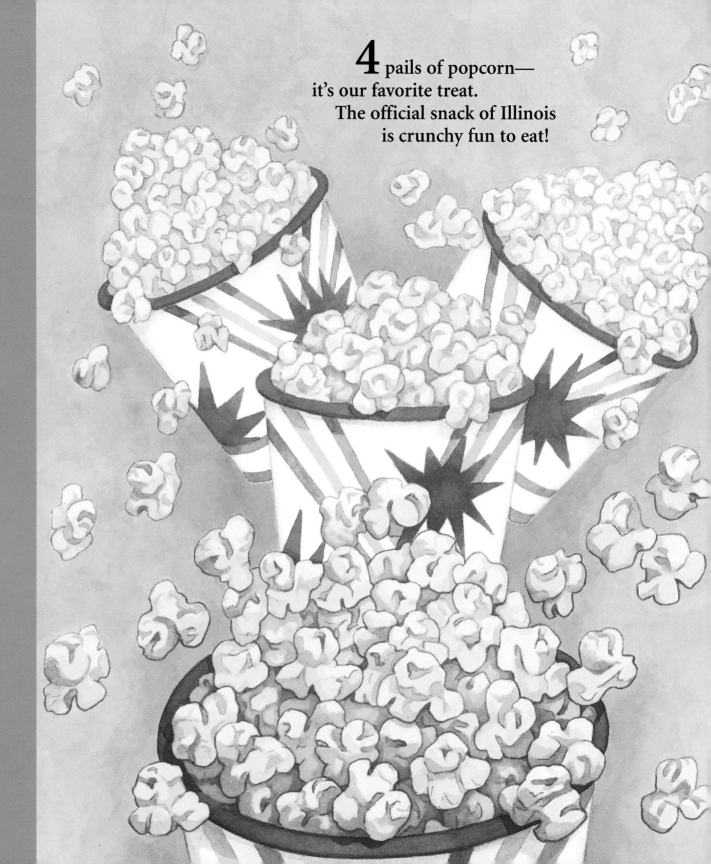

4 pails of popcorn—
it's our favorite treat.
The official snack of Illinois
is crunchy fun to eat!

Illinois is one of the top corn producing states in the nation. *Zea mays* is the botanical name for corn and each plant contains a male and a female part. The ear is a female flower stalk, and its tiny silk hairs are visible during growth, while the male flower is the tassel at the top of the plant stalk. Pollination occurs when wind carries pollen from the tassels on some plants to the silks on others. Corn plants grow from seven to eight feet tall and are harvested using a combine. Most of that corn is used to make feed for livestock, but some is also used for making plastics, ethanol, and foods.

five

5

5 ears of sweet corn
growing in the sun.
Their golden tassels tell us when
it's time to pick each one.

Do you hear the music?
Square Dancers do-si-do.
Do you spot all **6** of them
twirling to and fro?

The Square Dance was designated as the American Folk Dance of Illinois in 1990. It developed as immigrants brought and shared their own unique style of national dance with others. In a square dance, couples, or groups of four couples, form a "square" while a "caller" hollers out the instructions to the participants as they are dancing. Traditionally such dances were accompanied by instruments such as the fiddle, banjo, guitar, and accordian.

six

6

7 zippers zipping
in the hands of girls and boys,
invented here in Illinois
and named so for their noise.

In 1851 a gentleman from the East named Elias Howe invented a device called the Automatic Continuous Clothing Closure. However, he failed to market this device and in 1893, Whitcomb Judson from Chicago patented his device, called the Clasp Locker. Shortly after, Judson and businessman Lewis Walker launched the Universal Fastener Company to manufacture this new device. In 1913 an employee produced a better model called the Separable Fastener, which was patented in 1917. This is the model we know today as the modern zipper. B. F. Goodrich Company used the zipper on a boot they were manufacturing and decided to call the device a zipper, because of the zipping sound it made.

seven

7

Mazon Creek Fossils can be found in a type of rock called Francis Creek Shale, located in the Mazon Creek area of Grundy, Will, Kankakee, and Livingston counties.

Over 300 million years ago, Illinois was a mix of swamp and shallow marine bays, and a tropical climate covered the area. Many unique plants and animals lived in this area and when they died, they fell to the bottom of the bay where they were quickly covered in mud. As bacteria began to decompose the plant or animal, carbon dioxide was produced nearby. This carbon dioxide mixed with iron in the water, resulting in a type of ironstone that further protected the remains. This rapid burial provided excellent preservation of not only the hard parts of plants or parts of animals such as bones, shells, or teeth, but also of soft-bodied animals that typically do not fossilize.

eight
8

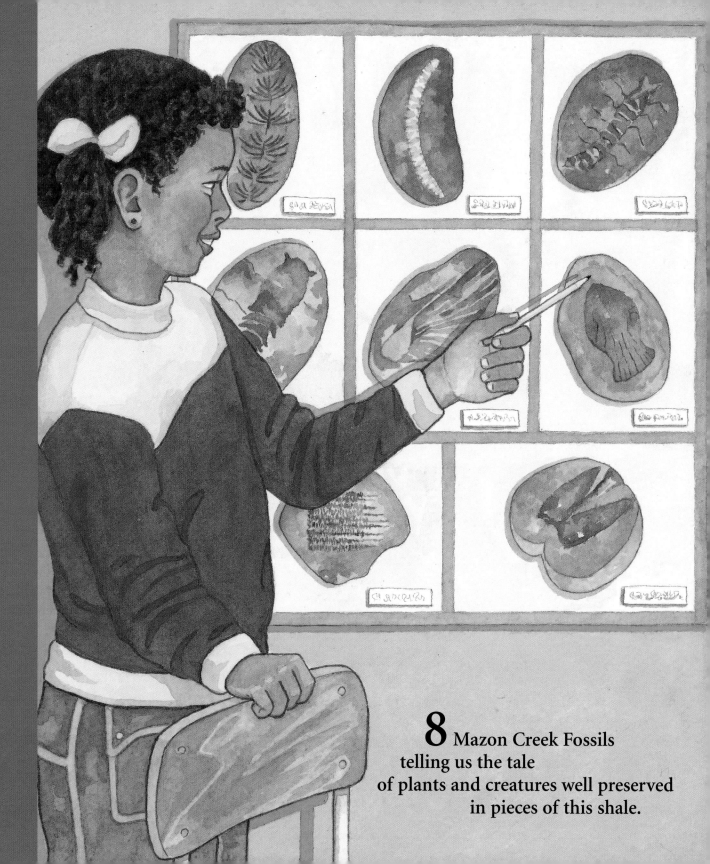

8 Mazon Creek Fossils
telling us the tale
of plants and creatures well preserved
in pieces of this shale.

Fluorite, derived from the Latin word *fluere*, which means to flow, was made the Official State Mineral of Illinois in 1965. Fluorite is a form of calcium fluoride, and is most often a transparent, glass-like mineral. Pure fluorite has no color, but impurities may cause it to appear in shades of violet, blue, yellow, or pink, or to even show bands of several colors. Illinois was once the largest producer of fluorite in the United States. Today most fluorite is imported from other countries. Because it melts easily, it is most commonly used as an ingredient to help lower the temperature during the process of making steel. It can also be found in household items such as toothpaste and optic lenses.

nine

9

9 bits of fluorite.
Have you ever seen
the Illinois State Mineral
in pink or blue or green?

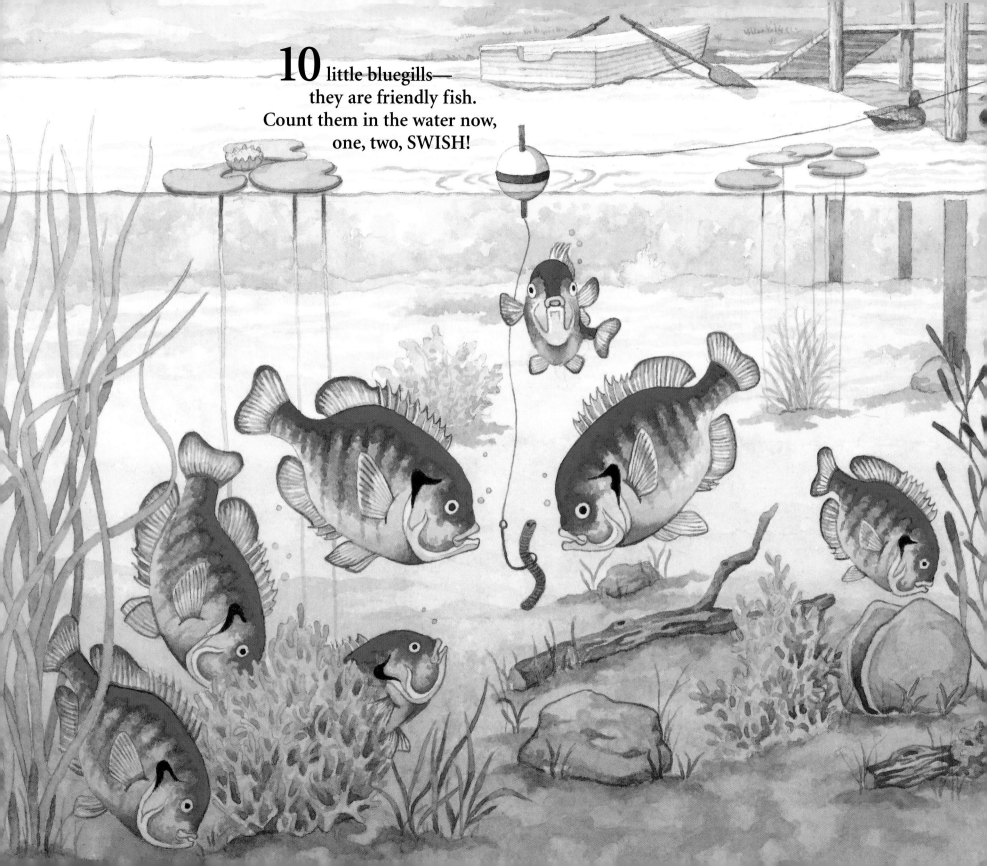

10 little bluegills—
they are friendly fish.
Count them in the water now,
one, two, SWISH!

The bluegill, or *Lepomis macrochirus*, is the Official State Fish of Illinois and a common species throughout the state. Occurring in a variety of habitats such as lakes, swamps, overflow ponds, and more, it will often live in a small school with up to 30 individual fish. A small- to medium-sized fish, the bluegill thrives on aquatic insects and larvae, but will also eat smaller fish, crayfish, snails, and sometimes algae.

ten

10

11 Illinois Chorus Frogs
living underground.
When they try to sing a song,
they make a bird-like sound.
Chirp! Chirp! Chirp!

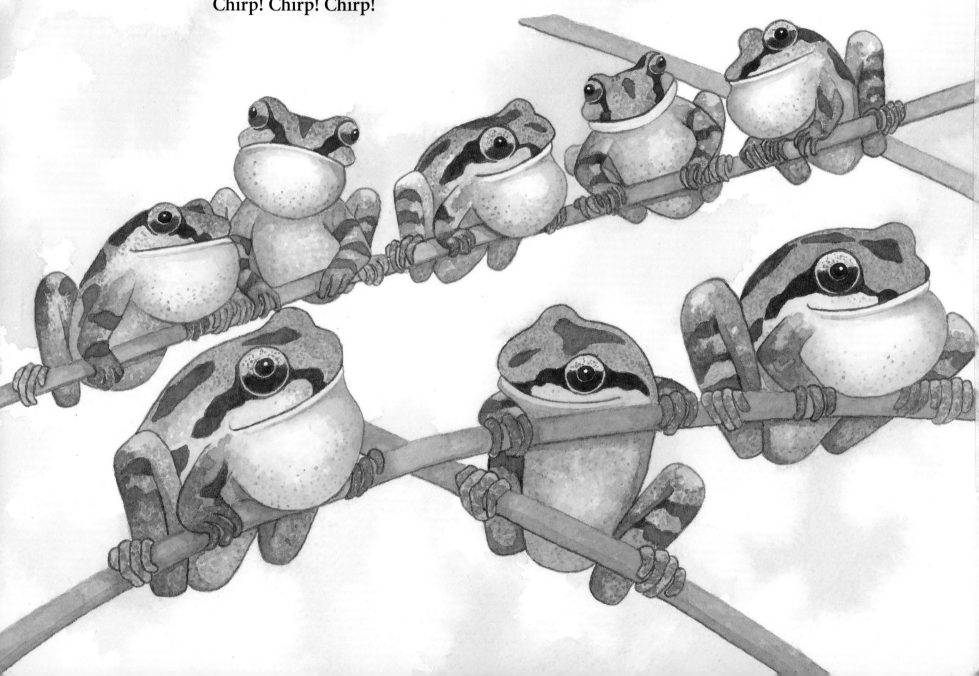

The Illinois Chorus Frog, or *Pseudacris streckeri illinoensis*, resembles a stout toad with thick forearms, which are used to dig burrows in the ground. A state threatened species in Illinois, it lives in open sandy areas such as former sandy prairie grasslands, and will live most of its life underground. The Illinois Chorus Frog emerges from its burrow during breeding time in late winter or during heavy summer rains to feed. The male has a distinct breeding call, which is a series of high-pitched, bird-like whistles.

eleven
11

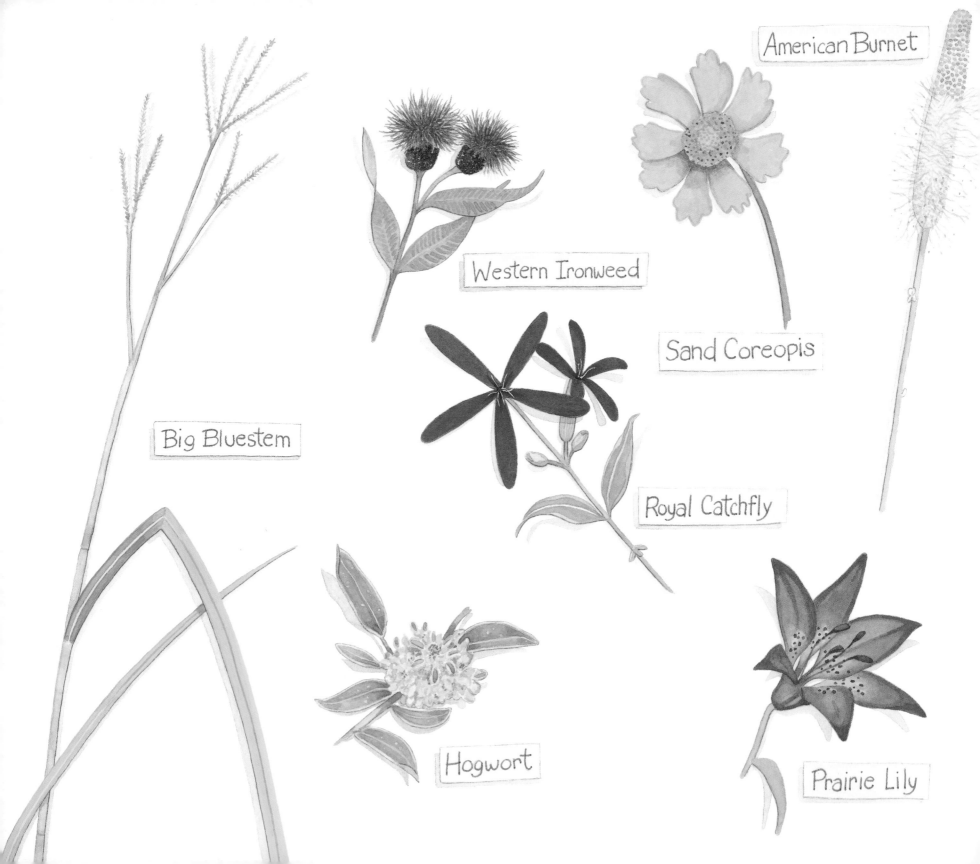

American Burnet

Western Ironweed

Sand Coreopis

Big Bluestem

Royal Catchfly

Hogwort

Prairie Lily

Downy Gentian

Black-Eyed Susan

Prairie Trout Lily

False Garlic

Sensitive Briar

In the early 1800s, most of Illinois was covered by a vast tallgrass prairie, a 22-million-acre (about 9-million hectare) ecosystem of grass and wildflowers. This flat, slightly rolling land with few trees made good farmland and soon became a natural choice for farmers to plow. By the end of the 1800s, very little of the natural prairie remained. Prairie wild-flowers and grass such as big bluestem, black-eyed Susan, and downy gentian are prairie favorites. Today only frag-ments of this prairie remain, and it is important that we preserve these areas and plant new prairies where we can.

twelve

12

12 native prairie flowers.
We must learn to care.
Every patch of prairie land
is beautiful and rare.

While several towns lay claim to having created the idea of serving ice cream in a dish with toppings, Evanston, Illinois claims to have named the treat "sundae." In the late 1800s, many types of treats such as ice-cream sodas were banned on Sunday in order to "keep the Sabbath day holy." To still have a treat, a local drugstore offered an ice-cream soda without the soda, and named it the ice-cream sundae.

20 ice-cream sundaes
named in Illinois.
Scoop the ice cream in a dish,
add toppings and enjoy!

30 people standing
and waiting just to say
that from the top of Sears Tower
they see miles away!

Taking three years to build, the Sears Tower was completed on May 3, 1973. One hundred ten stories and the world's tallest building at time of completion until 1996, the structure rises to a height of 1,450 feet tall. It is one of the most recognized buildings in the world and from its sky deck you can see four states on a clear day: Illinois, Indiana, Wisconsin, and Michigan.

thirty
30

In 1920 A. E. Staley of the Staley Starch Company founded the Decatur Staley's and hired George Halas to play, organize, and coach the team. Later that year Halas met with representatives from 11 other teams and organized the American Professional Football Association, which eventually became the NFL. In 1921 Halas and his co-head coach, Dutch Sternaman, assumed ownership of the team, and in 1922 they renamed them the Chicago Bears.

40 Decatur Staley Bears
ready for the game.
Our first professional football team,
later changed their name.

50 pretty paintings
hanging on the wall
in our famous art museums
Can you count them all?

Illinois is known for its cultural attractions such as The Art Institute of Chicago, Adler Planetarium and Astronomy Museum, Museum of Contemporary Art, Museum of Science and Industry, the Chicago Cultural Center, and many more. The Art Institute of Chicago was founded in 1879 as a school and museum and had the vision to acquire works of all kinds and conduct educational art programs. The Chicago Cultural Center was completed in 1897 and serves as one of the most comprehensive free arts centers in the United States, which means there are admission-free programs and exhibitions nearly every day of the year.

fifty
50

Illinois' various soil types enable farmers to grow and raise many animals and crops such as cattle, wheat, soybeans, corn, and more. With more than 76,000 farms, beef cows can be found on nearly 23 percent of those farms, while dairy cows are found on approximately 3 percent.

sixty
60

Now it's time for counting cows
They are saying "Moo!"
Can you count to **60**?
It's so much fun to do!

Do you see the butterflies
filling up the sky?
We must count to **70**
before they all float by.

The Argos Skipper is an endangered species in Illinois. Its wings are yellowish orange with black borders, which are wider on females. Their caterpillars live on big bluestem grass and other grasses, and adults thrive in the natural prairie habitat of Canada thistle, dogbane, purple coneflower, and ox-eye daisies.

seventy

70

Illinois is currently one of our nation's top pork producers, which is a major contributor to the state's economy. This industry contributes nearly 2 billion dollars to the Illinois economy each year through pork production, feed, equipment, transportation, and processing. The pork industry is also one of the largest consumers of grain. There are many different breeds of pigs including Hampshire, Yorkshire, Landrace, and more.

eighty
80

80 hogs playing
and squealing in the mud.
One hog rolls over,
one sits down with a thud.

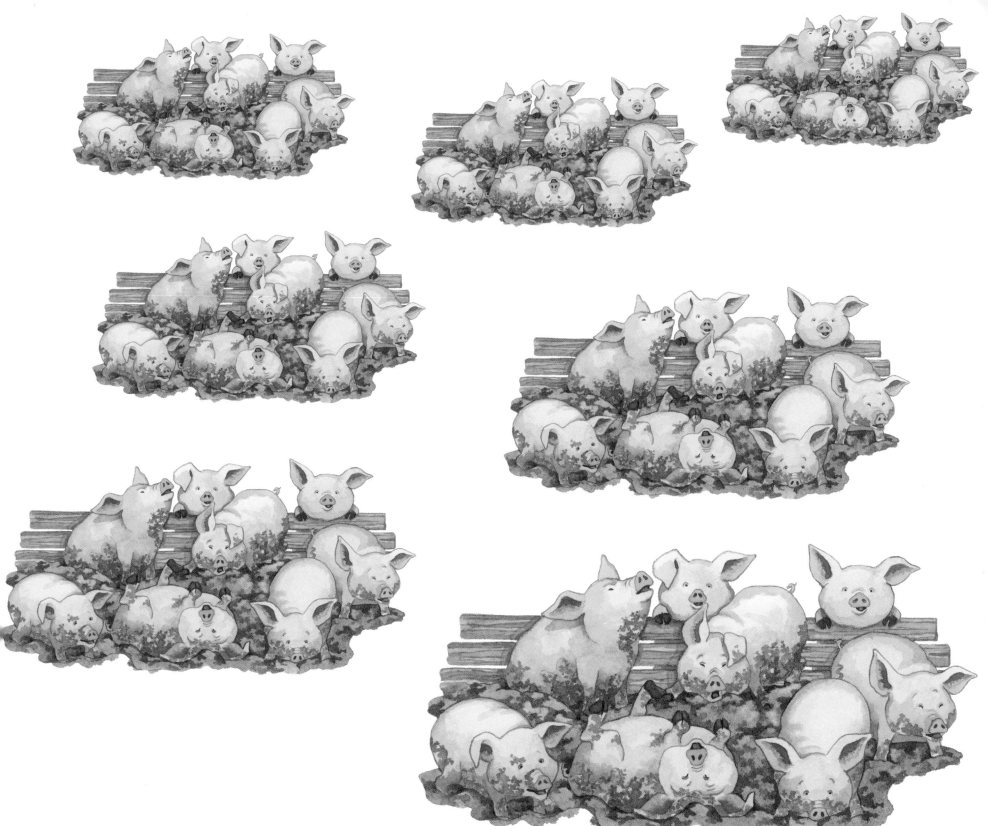

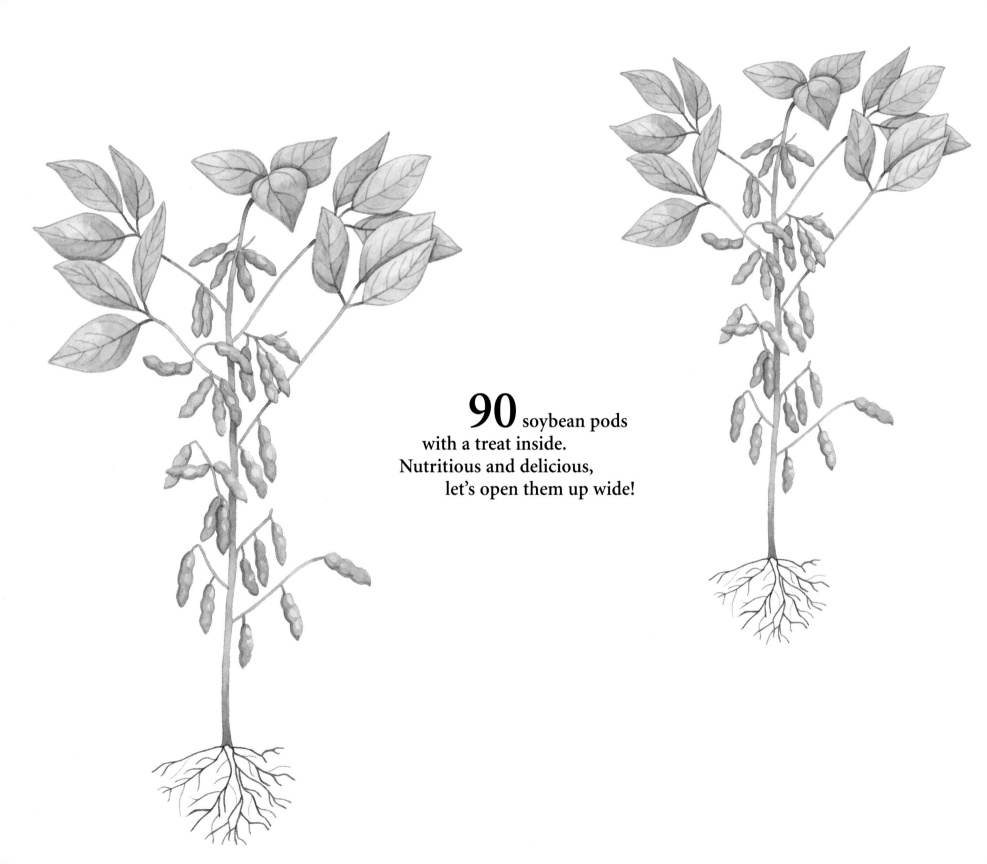

90 soybean pods
with a treat inside.
Nutritious and delicious,
let's open them up wide!

Illinois ranks second in the nation for the production of soybeans, a foremost provider of protein and oil. A relative to clover, peas, and alfalfa, the soybean plant flowers in the summer with approximately 60 or more pods per plant, each pod containing three small soybeans. Soybeans are used as whole beans, soybean meal, or soybean oil. Some interesting uses range from cooking oil to ink, milk products to plastic, and diesel fuel to adhesives. When eaten whole, whether baked, toasted, or boiled, soybeans are a tasty and healthy treat.

ninety
90

The Hine's Emerald Dragonfly, or *Somatochlora hineana*, is one of the most endangered dragonflies in the country and was listed as a state endangered species in Illinois in 1991. The adult Hines Emerald Dragonfly has green eyes and a dark brown and metallic green thorax, distinguished by two yellow lateral lines. Its larval habitat depends on cool, shallow, slow-moving waters such as spring-fed marshes and channels. Destruction of its habitat by urbanization is one of the main contributing reasons for its decline.

one hundred 100

100

Lovely little dragonflies
soaking up the sun.
wait for counting.
Hooray, let's say "We're done!"

Kathy-jo Wargin

Kathy-jo Wargin is the author of many bestselling books for children such as *L is for Lincoln: An Illinois Alphabet*, an IRA Teacher's Choice Award Winner; *The Legend of the Loon*, an IRA Children's Choice Award Winner; *Win One for The Gipper*; *The Edmund Fitzgerald: Song of the Bell*; as well as *The Legend of Sleeping Bear*; *A Mother's Wish*; and many more.

She lives in Petoskey, Michigan with her husband, nature photographer Ed Wargin, and their son. They live on three acres with two dogs, fifteen visiting white-tailed deer, nine wild turkeys, three passing coyotes, and one very busy red-tailed hawk.

Kathy O'Malley

Kathy O'Malley knew she wanted to be an artist from the age of six. Kathy graduated from Chicago's Columbia College, and has illustrated more than 39 children's books. Her work can also be found on greeting cards, gift bags, limited-edition collectibles, and decorative home products. She works from her home studio overlooking her perennial gardens, watched by two loyal art critics, her spoiled standard poodles. See more of Kathy's illustrations at: www.kathyomalley.com.